R.E.W.A.R.D.

Restoring Every Woman's Adrenaline Rush to Disciple

Developed by Rev. Sharon D. Jones
(An International Kingdom Women's Coalition, Inc. Project)

R.E.W.A.R.D.

Copyright © 2015 by Sharon D. Jones

All rights reserved. No part of this book may be reproduced, stored in retrieval system, or transmitted in any form or by any means – electronic, mechanical, photocopy, recording, or otherwise – without written permission of the author.

Unless otherwise noted, Scripture is taken from the HOLY BIBLE, King James Version. The King James Version (KJV) is in the public domain. Scripture quotations marked "MSG" or "The Message" are taken from The Message. Copyright 1993, 1994, 1995, 1996, 2000, 2001, 2002. Used by permission of NavPress Publishing Group http://www.navpress.com/

Copyedited by Sarah Gardner

ISBN: 978-0-9964040-2-0

Library of Congress Control Number (LLCN): 2015949026

Published by Kingdom Kaught Publishing LLC, Odenton, MD

First Printing 2015
Printed in the United States

Acknowledgments

First, I want to thank my Heavenly Father who knows all things and orchestrates everything for our good and His glory. As Psalm 37:23 says, "...*steps are ordered by the Lord*..."

Next, I want to thank my pastor and supportive husband, Dr. Aaron R. Jones. I have always had great joy in pushing his visions, but each time he would ask me "What is mine?" Although I didn't have an answer, he always encouraged me to seek the Lord to find it. As soon as I shared *R.E.W.A.R.D.* with him, he became my advertiser. I so LOVE him!

Finally, I want to thank my International Kingdom Women's Coalition (IKWC) sisters. IKWC is a collage of powerful women who willingly come together (both nationally and internationally) to serve and be served by taking each other's vision to the next level. In doing so, we form relationships we may otherwise have never had the opportunity to begin. We are women who acknowledge that we have much to share, and much to gain through an open exchange of new and valuable information. We provide a collaboration of resources using modern technology to reach nations; and, therefore advance the Kingdom of God. Together, we make it possible for a woman to realize her own goals, potential, and dreams.

Table of Contents

Preface 1
Introduction 5
Chapter 1: *What is R.E.W.A.R.D.?* 9
Chapter 2: *The Initial Reaction* 17
Chapter 3: *Women in a Safe Place: Looking at Yourself* 29
Chapter 4: *Laughing at Myself* 39
Chapter 5: *Pamper Me* 47
Chapter 6: *A Night of Laughter* 57
Chapter 7: *Thankful for You* 65
Chapter 8: *You are My Gift* 73
Chapter 9: *Restored to Disciple* 79
About the Developer 83

Preface

A few months prior to being introduced to International Kingdom Women's Coalition (IKWC), I was desperately searching for a conference for pastors' wives and/or women serving in fulltime ministry. My husband and I had been serving as pastors for over two years, and of course with growth come challenges, and with challenges come the feeling of overwhelm-ness. I don't like feeling overwhelmed (especially for a long period of time). I sent text messages to two of my good friends (who are pastors' wives) to ask "Why aren't there any local conferences for pastors' wives and women in ministry?" Of course they didn't have an answer to my question. I said to the Lord, "There must be a group or place where we can go to express our concerns confidentially (and not be judged), release the stress, and be restored back to serve in ministry."

A month or so later, I received a letter from the founder and visionary of IKWC. The letter introduced the vision of IKWC. I thought, "I will check this out; maybe this will be the avenue for me to get my release." As I attended the initial IKWC meeting, I listened to the founder share her vision of Christian women empowering other Christian women (locally and globally). She stated that God has birthed something in each one of us, and whether we serve in the marketplace or in fulltime ministry, God wants us to share our story. Oddly, she kept referencing me reaching other pastors' wives as an example. At the end of the meeting, I thought, "Lord, is this the avenue to meet other pastors' wives and women in ministry?"

In the fall of 2012, IKWC invited a brand and marketing consultant to teach us about "Identifying Your Why." A few days after the presentation, we were given 10 questions to answer to help us "identify our why." As I answered each question, I noticed that I had a passion to aid in the well-being of pastors' wives and women in ministry. I wanted to know if these women were experiencing similar challenges, and their methods of dealing with them. Little did I know that the Lord was preparing the way for R.E.W.A.R.D. Yes, I know Habakkuk 2:2 says, *"...write the vision...that he may run that reads it."* I never expected this vision to run, and so swiftly.

Preface

In January 2013, all the IKWC charter members voted on a vision. Surprisingly, my vision and another member's vision were tied for first place. I was SPEECHLESS when the other person conceded and everyone agreed to support my vision! With the encouragement and excitement of my IKWC sisters, we gathered profile information of each charter member (e.g. birth dates, likes/dislikes, hobbies, etc.) and scheduled our first R.E.W.A.R.D. activity.

R.E.W.A.R.D.

Restoring Every Woman's Adrenaline Rush to Disciple

Introduction

The greatest threat to a woman is the lack of balance. A woman's day is consumed with family, work, and her own personal obligations. Every day, a woman is preoccupied with balancing her life along with the lives of those who are connected to her (i.e. spouse, children, parents, etc.). The word *balance* is defined as "to keep or to put something in a steady position so that it does not fall; to offset or to compare the value of one thing with another."

Serving in ministry is another aspect of balance that many women have to add to their plate of obligations. Ministry is a servant assignment. It is an extension of the love of God. Jesus said to His disciples in Mark 10:43, *"...but whosoever will be great among you, shall be your minister (servant)."* Embracing this valuable assignment, oftentimes, means self-sacrifice. And because women are nurturers by nature, they tend to over-extend themselves to ensure that others receive the best. The result is a quick burnout and emotional frustration.

This emotional frustration can lead to depression, illness, death, and/or complications in the family and the church.

R.E.W.A.R.D. is developed to help women who serve in ministry (i.e. full-time, part-time, pastors' wives, etc.) relax, relate, release, and be restored. Because these women become all things to all people, they are never given the time or the opportunity to find a reprieve for themselves. According to a 2010-2014 statistic by Daniel Sherman, author of *Pastor Burnout Workbook,* it stated the following:

{1} 40% of pastors and 47% of spouses are suffering from burnout, frantic schedules, and/or unrealistic expectations.
{2} 45% of pastors' wives say the greatest danger to them and their family is physical, emotional, mental, and spiritual burnout.
{3} 52% of pastors say they and their spouses believe that being in pastoral ministry is hazardous to their family's well-being and health.
{4} 56% of pastors' wives say that they have no close friends.

Introduction

Hearing my heart and seeing the vision, the IKWC charter members agreed to be recipients of this pilot project. They all agreed at the introductory meeting that once they are healed and made whole, they will be able to encourage other women to attend a R.E.W.A.R.D. session.

R.E.W.A.R.D.

Restoring Every Woman's Adrenaline Rush to Disciple

Chapter 1: *What is R.E.W.A.R.D.?*

R.E.W.A.R.D. is a Christ-centered venue created for women who serve in ministry. This venue can be in a home, a public setting, or a weekend get-a-way. These venues are safe and empowering. The purpose for the venue is to help these women find a way to relax, to relate, to release, and to be restored back to building God's Kingdom.

R.E.W.A.R.D. does not demand anything of its members, but a willing-heart and the willingness to sacrifice time to find refuge and restoration. There are three levels to R.E.W.A.R.D.:

Level 1 - **IMMEDIATE** – Women making themselves available to talk to other women who serve in ministry. This is one-on-one communication (via phone, email, webcam, etc.) to share and discuss what is on each heart. The Bible encourages seeking "wise counsel."

Level 2 – **INTERMEDIATE** – Women making themselves available to have a meal with other women who serve in ministry. Meals can be at home or at a public setting. This relaxed setting should provide two or more women an open opportunity to build relationships without ministry talk! There is something about "breaking bread" that welcomes open-conversation and relaxation at the same time.

Level 3 - **ADVANCE** – Women making themselves available to go on a mini-vacation (2 days) with other women who serve in ministry. This is a time to really talk and glean from one another. This time allows everyone to relax, to fellowship, and to be restored. It is always good to "get-a-way and refresh" one's spirit.

All three venues require a high level of confidentiality, respect, and spiritual enrichment. The work of ministry involves one's physical, emotional, and spiritual well-being. Therefore, these venues are not to be used to insult or slander people (i.e. individuals, families, or parishioners). They are used for women to openly express themselves without being judged, but at

Chapter 1: What is R.E.W.A.R.D.?

the same time be replenished and restored in Christ. In the following chapters, you will read about IKWC's seven month *R.E.W.A.R.D.* experience.

How Refreshing?
By DN

My experiences through the many sessions of R.E.W.A.R.D. were very refreshing. The mere idea of being with a team of women of like passion, yet nurturing their personal and professional ministries of different calibers, strengths, abilities and characters, was enjoyable. The interactive, upfront and personal bonding with these women of God was actually enlightening. My perception of every session was that each was fruitful, creatively thought out, and well executed with Divine direction. I felt the need to hear the aspirations of others in ministry. I wanted to learn how they coped with the struggles and burdens of everyday life. How do they continue to carry the burden of a ministry to which their hearts are passionately pulled?

Women collectively seek to do this dual deed of family life and church life. The R.E.W.A.R.D. sessions allowed us, ladies, to relax and to be honest with ourselves and each other. We were surrounded by real people without the religious masks and make-up. This is not to say that we were without Christian character; quite the contrary. Much of our conversations were

Chapter 1: What is R.E.W.A.R.D.?

wholesome talk about everything. We laughed. We cried. We dined and we prayed. This was an atmosphere of openness, with full participation and a blossoming of individual personalities, gifts, and talents. We actually found our own inner-beauty within our sisters' beauty.

As I looked back on the year of *R.E.W.A.R.D.*, what I recalled was a year of unveiling our inner-selves. We were WOMEN comforting, empowering, and affirming WOMEN. I was especially excited about the flow of sharing our hearts. It is not often that we are afforded the time to think or talk about our likes and dislikes. We are more often doing what is required of us, and responding spontaneously. *R.E.W.A.R.D.* allowed us all to actually take a deep breath and exhale. The pleasure of knowing that there is a team of sisters behind you, pushing you upward, is exhilarating and of GOD. This support provides extra encouragement (without selfish-ambitions and vain conceit) with humility. This for me is the crux of *R.E.W.A.R.D.*

R.E.W.A.R.D. Moments

{1} Woman of God, when was the last time you have been refreshed (individually or corporately)?

{2} Woman of God, how do you "let your hair down?" How do you feel afterwards?

{3} Woman of God, is your way of refreshing being alone, being with family, or being with one of your sister-girls?

{4} Woman of God, do you have a good friend who is serving in ministry? A friend who lets you be you? A friend who encourages you and redirects you back to your God-ordained assignment?

Chapter 1: What is R.E.W.A.R.D.?

R.E.W.A.R.D. Prayer

Father, in the name of Jesus, I thank You for my sisters in ministry. I thank You for connecting me with women who will find the time to rest and to be refreshed in You. Lord, Your Word says in Proverbs 18:24, "A man that hath friends must shew himself friendly: and there is a friend that sticketh closer than a brother." Help me to be a good friend to other women in ministry. Help me to connect with sisters who have similar Godly passions as me. Once we have made the connection, help us to have a R.E.W.A.R.D. experience. I thank You in advance.

Amen.

R.E.W.A.R.D.

Restoring Every Woman's Adrenaline Rush to Disciple

Chapter 2: *The Initial Reaction*

After our initial meeting in which everyone chose to be a recipient of R.E.W.A.R.D.; I sought the Lord for our first activity. While all charter members may not be familiar with one another, they do have three things in common. They: 1) love the Lord Jesus; 2) serve in ministry; and 3) agree to be IKWC charter members. With these commonalities, there needs to be an activity that will cause the women to get to know one another, and at the same time develop a trust and respect for each other. I developed three interactive activities (Select & Respond; Keep or Give Away; and Scavenger Hunt) to address this need.

Activity 1 - Select & Respond

This activity was a challenge for many. Each woman selected a card and had to respond as the card instructed. Some asked if they could switch their card, but I told them the cards could not be switched. The questions on the cards caused the women to think and to be honest with themselves. Each woman was directed to stand facing the group to give answers. Although it was difficult, all the women were very transparent with their responses.

Activity 2 – Keep or Give Away

This activity involved the women partnering in pairs. There were three teams formed, and one woman per team was given the opportunity to choose a card. Based on the card's instruction, one woman could answer the questions or pass the card to her partner. Surprisingly, each woman who drew a card chose to keep it and respond. They all responded with excitement and appreciation. The group concluded that the questions were light-hearted and favorable.

Activity 3 – Scavenger Hunt

For the final activity, I gave the same team of women colored strips of paper. The color strips were used to identify x-number of color coded items to find together throughout a designated location. The intent of this activity was to establish relationships and to experience their initial reaction to the unknown. All team members had an exciting time together; some were strategic in their search, and others were random. But overall, their

Chapter 2: The Initial Reaction

response became more appreciative than their initial response in Activity 1.

At the end of the Scavenger Hunt, the women shared their initial reaction to each item they found. A majority of the women stated that the items were things that they love. One of the women stated that an item she found reminded her that it has been a while since she has taken a trip. She loves to travel. Another woman stated that purple is her favorite color, and the majority of the items she found were purple.

I closed the fellowship with Philippians 4:8, *"Finally, brethren, whatsoever things are true, whatsoever things are honest, whatsoever things are just, whatsoever things are pure, whatsoever things are lovely, whatsoever things are of good report; if there be any virtue, and if there be any praise, think on these things."* My final remark was, "Our initial reaction to things that we do not like to do or talk about is usually negative or rejection, but our reaction to things we like is always favorable. Let's view everything according to this scripture."

One of the charter members stated that these activities caused her to open her heart to the others. She stated that some may need to go deeper in order to be healed, and all the members agreed. Therefore, it was a consensus that the next activity should encourage each one to explore her heart more and to close the door of brokenness.

The goal of *R.E.W.A.R.D.* is to make women whole and restored in Christ in order to better serve God's people. We joined hands and closed in prayer.

Chapter 2: The Initial Reaction

My Reflection
By WS

Initially, when each of us pulled a card, we didn't want to answer our question because we thought the answers would be too personal. We didn't really fully know or trust each other well enough to disclose that level of personal information. By the end of our meeting, we had become paired with a sister that we didn't know a lot about. But working together during the scavenger hunt enabled us to see how much we really had in common.

I felt at the beginning of the meeting that this would just be an ordinary exercise. We picked a card and were told to give feedback on the card. On the second round, we were given another card and the opportunity to choose whether to keep or pass it on. The majority of us decided to keep our cards. The feedback we gave caused us to be introspective. We found out that there were many things in the cards that spoke to our vulnerabilities, our likes, our dislikes, and the places we have come from in our lives. This caused us to open up to each other and build a level of confidence that had never been there before.

The scavenger hunt was where we really were able to get involved in getting to know one another by helping each other. Now that we had opened up a little bit more, we were willing to step into each other's personalities and giggle, hug, and really let down our guards. We each got excited in working to find something together on the list. It caused us to work together as a team. Many times, we as women go at it alone, not realizing that we really play an integral role in each other's lives. We learned what our partners like and they learned what we like. It makes me think that we were so focused on helping each other that we forgot about the fact that we really didn't know one another.

I looked at it as being like children who are first starting in a new class at a new school for the first time. Initially they are apprehensive about this new place. After all, they have become comfortable with mommy, daddy, and themselves. That is their world. Now it's time to move from that level of comfort and invite others to be a part of their new journey. They may come in and stand by the door for a minute, and then

Chapter 2: The Initial Reaction

slowly inch their way to the other children to participate in the group. An hour later, you may see them laughing, playing, and running around without a care in the world.

I believe this session was much like that. What started out as a "standing-at-the-door" moment, soon turned into a night of running around looking for the objects on our lists. We were laughing and giggling like kindergarteners without the inhibitions we had come there with. We had even taken off our shoes and gotten down on our hands and knees to help our sisters find things on their lists. Through this exercise, I discovered that we have the potential to let go and embrace the little girl inside all of us.

I walked away with more of a sense of closeness with these ladies-- especially my scavenger hunt partner. This was mutually helpful because it was later discovered that my partner had been diagnosed with breast cancer. Through our closeness, I saw how I had developed a true sense of sisterly love for her. I was able to pray and petition God for her healing as if she was my natural sister. I believe that the timing for this exercise was perfect and well designed by God. To this day, I love my sister friend more than she will ever know. The other ladies rallied around her as well, not in a feeling of pity for her, but in the true sense of sisterly love that was embraced by the entire group! True unity was established as a result.

I give glory to God for His movement and timing in causing these IKWC sessions to flow in the right order. He truly orchestrated this meeting! My sister friend is now healed and walking in Divine health. We all cried and embraced each other like never before. This led me to know that our Heavenly Father wants us to walk in unity because it is there that you can command the blessing!

Chapter 2: The Initial Reaction

R.E.W.A.R.D. Moments

{1} Do you like surprises? When was the last time you were caught off-guard? How did you respond?

{2} How transparent are you? Are you willing to share intimate details about yourself with other women in ministry who do not know you? If no, explain why.

{3} Looking at your life in ministry, does it sometimes feel like you are in a Scavenger Hunt (i.e. searching for peace of mind, a moment to yourself, or time to be you)?

{4} Read Philippians 4:8. Take five minutes to allow the Holy Spirit to minister to you. If it is longer than five minutes; it is okay. REMEMBER: You need a *R.E.W.A.R.D.* Experience!

R.E.W.A.R.D. Prayer

Father, I thank You for using this time to minister me. Thank You for showing me how to deal with the unexpected and the uncomfortable. Dear Lord, I know You want to help me find rest in You. Help me see, through my willingness to be transparent and open with other women in ministry, that I can truly be myself and not feel guilty. Help me be a good friend to another woman in ministry. I know we all need a sister's keeper. I thank You in advance for this R.E.W.A.R.D. experience.

Amen.

Chapter 2: The Initial Reaction

This page was intentionally left blank

R.E.W.A.R.D.

Restoring Every Woman's Adrenaline Rush to Disciple

Chapter 3: *Women in a Safe Place: Looking at Yourself*

I must say, after seeing the move of God and the transparency of the women, I truly sought the Lord for the next activity. I said to the Lord, "Father, I do not know what You are doing but I will walk with You through this process." Then He gave me the idea of using a cup or a mug to describe ourselves. At our next fellowship, I brought a large bag with cups and mugs gift wrapped. I also had cards with three topics listed. The card read, "Looking at the item you retrieved, describe yourself using one of the 3 topics:

1. How You Felt This Week
2. You and Your Ministry
3. You as an Individual (No Job or Ministry Title)"

Once again, the women and the Lord amazed me. Each woman stated that the cup/mug retrieved was very significant to her. Each woman openly shared on a deeper level. Each woman was able to see herself through the object. One woman stated that the mug was a reminder of a scripture the Lord spoke to her when He called her into fulltime ministry. She stated, based on the current season of her life, the mug was a great reminder that God has and will continue to take care of her.

The more the women talked, the safer the environment became for each. The women shared how much they really enjoy letting their hair down (living a life of normalcy). They shared how much they appreciated that time of tears and laughter. We joined hands and closed in prayer.

Chapter 3: Women in a Safe Place: Looking at Yourself

My Testimony
By DB

Growing up, we were taught an unspoken lesson: what goes on in the house does not get shared with anyone outside the house. Well, inside the house, I had three younger sisters, a father, and a mother. I grew up in a household where children were seen and not heard (and weren't encouraged to **openly** express ourselves and/or share thoughts, concerns, and ideas). It would have been seen as a sign of disrespect if one shared a thought when not prompted to do so. From my parents' point-of-view, this was considered normal. They were people who worked hard to provide for their family. This was the priority and they did that well. They are still the most responsible people I know.

The good news is that I had three younger sisters "in the house." Growing up, they were my best friends. For the most part, we shared everything -- secrets, dreams, talents and experiences; cried about failures, pain, and disappointments; laughed about everything and each other; and learned from each other. I thank God for my sisters! Growing up, I felt most comfortable with them. Our bond was extremely tight and I think they'd all agree that I still work at keeping a close bond with each of them because they are my original girlfriends.

I believe because of the closeness that we shared; I never sought or had a great need to seek close relationships with other females. Along the way, I had friendships that I treasured but I never felt a need to share with them my innermost secrets as females often do. Actually, I believed that my family was so different from everyone else's that I thought they would look at me differently; that my family would be judged; and that I'd be embarrassed. It is only through maturing and expanding my horizon that I learned that we are all more alike than not and that everyone's family has some form of dysfunction. No one is perfect and no family is perfect. It took me over 30 years to realize that. And though I know it, and have only shared with a very small circle of people, I still am most comfortable with keeping portions of my life to myself.

When the three women I consider my best friends shared openly and freely, I was amazed and eventually I began to open up. Because these poised, professional,

Chapter 3: Women in a Safe Place: Looking at Yourself

beautiful women (whom I admired) could share their past and present lives with me; unknowingly, they helped me to grow comfortable sharing portions of my life with them. I remember sharing information about my family with my friend of 12 years. We were on our way to a women's retreat. It wasn't until she said that she's known me for several years, and yet I had never shared some basic family dynamics until that moment. I had not considered it a big deal until I continued to reflect on her comment. On the way home from the retreat, we were both on a spiritual mountaintop, and she shared with me that she will pray that I would be "free" and not so guarded.

As I seek God to show me how to be free, He reveals with whom I can share and what I can share. That being said, when the IKWC Sisters understood that we needed to go to a "deeper place" or "go to a deeper level" I was quite concerned. The emoji 😳 comes to mind. I retreated to my shell, and was not sure how this was going to work for me.

I believe that as we continued to meet, it became easier to share and open up. I appreciate the levels of R.E.W.A.R.D. By the time we had reached this exercise, we had already participated in several meetings and shared on an immediate and intermediate level. We were naturally ready for a deeper level. We had established a degree of commitment, trust, care, concern, love, and common goals and mission. So I believe the atmosphere was set for sharing.

Chapter 3: Women in a Safe Place: Looking at Yourself

R.E.W.A.R.D. Moments

{1} Are you comfortable with others or are you wearing a mask?

{2} What secrets are you protecting?

{3} In what environment do you feel most safe to share? Why?

{4} With whom do you openly share?

{5} What experiences do you have that you can share and be a blessing to another woman?

R.E.W.A.R.D. Prayer

Father, in the Name of Jesus, I thank You for relationships. Your Word says in Proverbs 27:17, "As iron sharpens iron, so one person sharpens another." I thank You for the people that You have placed in my life. Lord, I pray that You will keep me surrounded with women who are trustworthy, loving, caring, and faithful. I thank You for the opportunity to listen to and learn from wise women. I pray for discernment to know with whom and when I am to openly share my experiences with other women.

Lord, let me never be ashamed of my journey because it is the journey that You will use to bless me, Your people, and to Your glory. And I know that all things work together for good to those who love You, Lord, and are called according to Your purpose (Romans 8:28). I thank You that I am free indeed. I love You and bless Your Name in all things.

Amen

Chapter 3: Women in a Safe Place: Looking at Yourself

This page was intentionally left blank

R.E.W.A.R.D.

Restoring Every Woman's Adrenaline Rush to Disciple

Chapter 4: *Laughing at Myself*

Based on the trust and comfort established from the last two activities, I sought the Lord about transitioning to Level 2 of R.E.W.A.R.D. (the Intermediate Level – Dinner with No Ministry Talk). We scheduled a dinner outing at a local restaurant. I used the IKWC fact sheet about each charter member. This sheet listed each member's contact information; their likes and dislikes; and their favorites (food, colors, and activities).

I purchased each woman's favorite candy or colored item. I established seating based on the favorite items. Each woman approached their seat in amazement and with excitement. Two of the women sat down and grabbed hold of their candy. You should have seen their faces!!

Later in the evening, I had each woman share one of their most embarrassing moments. Each woman shared and we all laughed in tears. We had such a good time that the women chose to share two moments! The environment was so relaxing and enjoyable that the women transitioned from laughing at themselves to sharing ministry aspirations. The conversations were so enlightening that no one wanted to leave. A female waitress was so blessed by the fellowship that she joked about sitting down and joining us. The night ended with some of the women sharing their candy treats with the waitress.

As you can see Level 2 of R.E.W.A.R.D. was accomplished: a relaxed setting that provides women an open opportunity to know one another and also foster relationships with no ministry agenda.

Chapter 4: Laughing at Myself

My Testimony
By SJ

You have heard serious-minded people say, "It's not that funny!" And they usually say it with an agitated or disgruntled look on their faces. Depending on the situation, I may agree with them. Quite often, some things (even the most embarrassing things) are funny. If you are not laughing, then you are crying. Serving in ministry can cause you to do one or the other.

Because I have ministry talk, it seems like 24/7, I seize those moments to talk about something else. Usually that something else is something lighthearted and humorous. I don't know about you, but I laugh at myself often. I laugh at the many thoughts that go through my mind. I laugh at scenarios that I find myself in and trying to find a way of escape. If I do something embarrassing, like many, I look around to see if anyone else noticed it.

With that said, it was a BLAST listening to my IKWC Sisters sharing their embarrassing moments with no shame. We all could identify with one another with no pretense. You know as well as I do, that NEVER happens with women! Especially for women who are ministers of the gospel.

For some reason, we have been trained to be serious and have deep spiritual talks. Please do not misunderstand me, I LOVE talking about Jesus! I can talk about Jesus for hours. But Jesus conversations and church (ministry) talks are totally different. When I talk about Jesus, I leave encouraged, inspired, and compelled to draw closer to Him. When I talk about church (ministry), I may leave grieved, overwhelmed, and concerned about the body of Christ.

That's why I tell my sisters in ministry, beforehand, "No ministry talk tonight. Let's be free and laugh." They understand and wholeheartedly agree with me. I believe it makes for a R.E.W.A.R.D. night. And that's what took place at our night of "Laughing at Myself," we LAUGHED SO HARD that it compelled another woman to desire to join us.

Chapter 4: Laughing at Myself

R.E.W.A.R.D. Moments

{1} Woman of God, how often do you laugh at yourself? Are you laughing alone or are others laughing with you?

{2} Have you ever shared your most embarrassing moments with other women in ministry? What was the outcome?

{3} When was the last time you broke bread with another sister in ministry? What did you talk about (ministry, family, self, aspirations)? List them.

{4} Can you spend hours with another woman in ministry and not talk about church work **(REMEMBER: Talking about the goodness of Jesus is not the same thing)?**

R.E.W.A.R.D. Prayer

Dear Lord, I love to laugh. Throughout scripture, You have shown your servants laughing at a circumstance involving them. A few of them have even laughed at promises You have made to them. You said in Proverbs 17:22, "A merry heart doeth good like a medicine: but a broken spirit drieth the bones." As ministry becomes intense and demanding, help me to find time to laugh with a sister in the gospel. I don't want to become dry and bitter while serving Your people. I want the joy of You to always be my strength (Nehemiah 8:10). I thank You in advance.

Amen

Chapter 4: Laughing at Myself

This page was intentionally left blank

R.E.W.A.R.D.

Restoring Every Woman's Adrenaline Rush to Disciple

Chapter 5: *Pamper Me*

Since time and schedules were not permitting us to go away for a few days to experience Level 3 of R.E.W.A.R.D. (Advanced), I decided to have a night of pampering at the home of a charter member. I invited a woman who specializes in massage therapy to pamper the group. We enjoyed an evening of hands and feet pampering as a spa-sound CD played throughout the night. The women were totally relaxed and enjoyed the night together. Two of the charter members were so blessed by the massage therapist's services that they pampered her. The therapist stated that in her 30 years of service, she has never had clients treat her to pampering! This was another night where no one rushed to leave.

R.E.W.A.R.D.'s Level 3 was accomplished: the women left replenished and restored in Christ. The women left ready to serve. Although this level requires a sacrifice of time, the pamper night showed that it was worth it.

My Testimony
By WS

I have always been uncomfortable with being touched. Even as a young girl, I was always taught to be guarded with my body, my thoughts, what I said, where I went, and how I would be perceived. My space was always considered personal. Being one of five daughters of a minister, we could never be open in fear that it would somehow bring shame to our parents, the church and/or God. I therefore grew up to be an adult with issues about being touched. It was hard to allow people to get close to me. That was an uncomfortable place for me! I could help others, but somehow I felt uncomfortable and vulnerable when it came to receiving that same help from others.

In this particular exercise, a lady was bought in to pamper us. She gave us hand and foot massages. As she massaged our feet, she began to quietly pray over us. Of course, as I contemplated having her touch my hands and feet, the sense of anxiety and dread began to overflow me. As I always do when I am nervous, I laughed and joked so as to not let anyone know that

Chapter 5: Pamper Me

this was an uncomfortable situation for me. However, I soon realized, there was no getting around this session. My mind raced as I pondered, what will she think of my feet? After all, they are ugly. Will she laugh? Will she touch them but really inwardly think of how hideous I am? Does she really want to be this close to me......with all of my flaws? I could definitely see how she could embrace the other ladies, but not me. After all, they deserve this session more than me.

After everyone else was finished, I finally sat in her chair to be pampered. As she began to work on my hands and pray over them, the Holy Spirit began to speak very gently through her to my inner thoughts and fears. The Holy Spirit and the soft, relaxing spa music helped to drown out the self-critical voices that had kept me in such a guarded state for so many years. I began to slowly realize that these are all the thoughts that I had imagined in my own mind. This is how I thought God felt about me. How would my heavenly Father want to touch me, as scarred as I am? Life had dealt me many harsh blows since childhood, so my heart in many ways was hard and calloused just like my feet. I had tried to fit in so many places only to find that I wasn't accepted because maybe I was too big, too small, too young, too old, too educated, not smart enough, not the right gender, not the right timing, not pretty enough, etc.

Just like my feet, I felt the pain from trying to fit in had disfigured me. And worse still, I felt that everyone in the room was now looking and judging my life based on the ugliness of my feet. But, oh, when I sat in the chair I was somehow willing to let go of every critical thought and conclusion I had of myself and that others may have had of me. It was refreshing for me to see that I could be touched by my sisters in ministry without being judged! Most of all, I felt more at ease to actually allow God to minister to me and receive wave upon wave of His unconditional love.

YOU ARE GOOD ENOUGH!

This exercise allowed me to face my insecurities head on and be all right with them. It also allowed me to realize that just as I can minister to others, I can also be ministered to and receive everything God has for me as well! I then realized that it was the voice of the enemy in my mind saying to me that I was not good enough to receive God's best. I am free today and I

Chapter 5: Pamper Me

am constantly reminded that "I am good enough." We are all marred vessels but God does His best work with vessels that become moldable in His hands. I am no longer afraid to let others see my flaws. I am free to allow the love of God to permeate my relationships. This experience allowed me to finally let others in. Hallelujah! I trust God more with me now. I believe that when we as women trust God with our whole being, He will never fail us and we will know that **WE ARE GOOD ENOUGH!**

LEARNING TO RECEIVE

I believe that women give out so very much that they may not realize that they must take time out to receive the R.E.W.A.R.D. that God has for them. We give to our spouses, our children, our parents, our jobs, and our ministries. We are often last on the receiving line. And when we do, most of the time there is that inner voice that nags at us telling us that it's not our time to receive. When Jesus washed the disciples' feet, He was clearly setting an example of not only how to serve but also how to receive. It is in receiving that we become refreshed and renewed for discipleship to others. It is in receiving that we respect the giver and his gift.

Relationships are indicative of a place called intimacy. Intimacy will cause a relationship to suffer when there is only a giver and not a receiver. It will never be fruitful. God gives us revelation as we give Him worship. He receives worship and we receive revelation and strategies for our lives. We then can birth the next level of our lives. Therefore, in order to birth anything there must be a giver and a receiver. These positions are, at times, interchangeable. If you are to birth your destiny, both parts are necessary. Ladies, you have been giving and now it is your time to receive!

Chapter 5: Pamper Me

R.E.W.A.R.D. Moments

{1} Is it hard for you to trust others? Why?

{2} Is it difficult for you to receive? Why?

{3} What opinion of yourself do you have?

{4} Are they self-imposed? Why?

{5} What is God's opinion of you?

R.E.W.A.R.D. Prayer

Dear Lord, You have given us all things that pertain to life and Godliness. Please help me to receive Your pampering. You died for our sins, so therefore You thought we were good enough! I receive Your thoughts about me…..to prosper me and give me an expected end. Jeremiah 29:11 says," For I know the thoughts and plans that I have for you," says the Lord, "thoughts and plans for welfare and peace and not for evil, to give you hope in your final outcome."

Lord, I trust You with my insecurities! As I bring them to You, I receive Your waves upon waves of unconditional love in my inner being in order to be a whole woman!

Amen.

Chapter 5: Pamper Me

This page was intentionally left blank

R.E.W.A.R.D.

Restoring Every Woman's Adrenaline Rush to Disciple

Chapter 6: *A Night of Laughter*

Understanding how much these women enjoy one another's company and do not mind laughing, I thought of Proverbs 17:22, *"A merry heart doeth good like a medicine..."* Therefore, I planned a game night at the same charter member's home. I brought two games to play, but we only played one: *Logo*.

There were two teams of three. Using the timer in the game, each team had a certain amount of time to act out or draw logos before the time ended. The women had a "gut busting" good time laughing at one another. Initially one of the women stated that she doesn't play games, but after the night was over she admitted that she enjoyed herself. Again, it was another late night and the women were in no rush to leave.

My Testimony
By YC

I am the woman who said, "I don't play games." It wasn't until after spending time with this group of loving and caring women that I took the time to think about why I didn't like playing games. I had never really given it much thought before; it was just something I didn't enjoy doing as a teenager or as an adult.

As I reflected back over my life, I remembered as a child I enjoyed playing hide and seek, jaxs, and hop scotch with my cousins and my girlfriends. So, it's not as though I never enjoyed playing games; it's that 'life' changed my perspective on having fun. In my early teens, my life changed drastically; my mother passed away. I watched her suffer with bone cancer for a number of years. She lost weight, lost her sight, and was bedridden for a number of years. As a young girl, along with the assistance of one my older sisters, I did the best I could to assist in taking care of my mother; then she died. There were times that I felt I had died along with her. I forgot how to laugh and have fun for

Chapter 6: A Night of Laughter

quite some time. I definitely didn't want to play games. Everything about life became serious to me.

After her passing, I was thrust into the position of taking care of my younger brother and sister, in addition to going to school. I cooked, cleaned, shopped for groceries, did the laundry, and paid the bills, while deeply grieving the loss of my mother. Games - who had time to play games? Who had time to play and laugh? I was pushed into a place of having a lot of responsibilities at an early age. I forgot how to be a teenager and how to have fun. Those things were no longer a part of my life. There was an expectation that someone had to step in to help keep things going, and at the time it was me.

I graduated from high school on a Friday, and on Saturday morning I was in route to Washington, D.C. to look for a job. In September of that year, I was hired for my first government position at a very prestigious organization. Within a couple of years I was promoted and with each and every position I occupied, I took on more and more responsibilities. I was groomed to work hard, to have the serious conversations with people, and that included upper management. I felt I couldn't play because I needed to ensure that people took me seriously. I was task-oriented and results-driven. I was serious about everything I did and everything I said. I felt that this definitely wasn't the time to play games, because my career and livelihood were involved. I surely wasn't going to run the risk of losing everything that I was working so hard for. Games, this surely wasn't the time to play!

This serious nature was at the heart of who I was so, of course, it flowed into my personal and intimate relationships. Because of my serious temperament and my no nonsense demeanor, older men were always attracted to me. Since I wasn't into playing games, I didn't take the time to enjoy dating younger men because I felt "who had time for young, foolish games?" I loved hard and didn't have time to play. Because I was always trying to find my footing in grown up relationships, I took life, and probably myself, much too seriously. I was stimulated and motivated by what I considered to be a mature and grown up life. I wasn't playing games because life wasn't play – it was serious to me. In hindsight, the intensity of how I lived really stole my joy and my laughter.

Chapter 6: A Night of Laughter

Then one day my life took another major change; I surrendered my heart to God. I still didn't play games but I learned how to be at peace, how to laugh and how to enjoy life. My perspective on being serious took on a different meaning. I was serious about wanting to know more about the God over my life; about the purpose and plans He has for me; and about what I could do to serve others. He placed people around me who knew how to enjoy being at peace with their relationship with Him. So, in turn, I began to relax and enjoy this space and time in my life.

Then one night this group of ladies decided to play games, and I think I had more fun than anyone else. I laughed with them and at myself. What a night of fun!! I realized how healthy laughter can be and that life is only as serious as I make it. Now, I have a new perspective – let the games begin!!!

R.E.W.A.R.D. Moments

{1} Have you allowed the challenges of life to steal your laughter?

{2} Are you too serious minded?

{3} When was the last time you played a game?

{4} Are you so focused on the task at hand that you missed out on the journey?

{5} Do you know the foundation for real joy and laughter?

{6} Are you at peace in your life?

Chapter 6: A Night of Laughter

R.E.W.A.R.D. Prayer

Lord God, in the Name of Jesus, thank You for the gift of laughter! I thank You for the joy You bring into my life through the simple things that I sometimes take for granted – a bright sunny day, the smile of a friend, or a good night's sleep. I thank You that You didn't let the challenges of life destroy me. I am so grateful that I know You – that You are holy and sovereign and righteous and just. You are loving and faithful and always good. Teach me to focus on You, Lord, not on myself or on my circumstances so I can live with a lighter, more joyful heart. Help me to remember that when I am looking up to You, I can have a more optimistic perspective about life and be a more positive person. I am so glad that I have a relationship with You, Lord because being connected to You I can have peace and joy. As Your peace covers me, the peace that passes all understanding, may it guard my heart and mind. I bless You, Lord, and I praise You.

Amen.

R.E.W.A.R.D.

Restoring Every Woman's Adrenaline Rush to Disciple

Chapter 7: *Thankful for You*

In lieu of meeting in November (due to the Thanksgiving holiday), I had the women draw names at the previous fellowship. I instructed the women, throughout the month of November, to send "I am thankful for you" messages to the woman whose name was drawn. The messages were sent via text, email, card, or Facebook. This exemplifies Level 1 of R.E.W.A.R.D. (Immediate), the one-on-one touch.

My Reflection
By YC

As women, we go about our daily lives taking care of our spouses, children, grandchildren, aging parents, and others. We are working inside and outside of the home, participating in church and social activities, and never really looking for anyone to tell us that they are thankful for who we are or for what we have done.

This activity gave us an opportunity to consider the things that we truly appreciate about our IKWC Sisters. Which before, I hate to admit, I hadn't given much thought. I knew there were a considerable number of characteristics that I admired about them; but if not for this activity, would I have ever told the person whose name I had drawn what I was thankful for about her? Probably not.

What is it about us, as women, that we don't take the time to acknowledge and give verbal or written thanks to the women who are a part of our lives? They give their time, energy, and love. They share valuable lessons learned from their life's experiences; and we often don't show our appreciation for who they are.

Chapter 7: Thankful for You

It's not that we don't appreciate them, we just don't verbalize it. This activity gave us a chance to change that and the impact was noteworthy.

At each meeting, we would all pour out ourselves in order to support the vision – giving but collectively leaving with more than what we came with. Always so thankful that we came together! This activity was more personal. We had a chance to hear what another person was thankful for regarding ourselves!

Giving thanks is the expression of gratitude, and gratitude is one of the most beautiful secrets in spiritual living. One of the most endearing things a person can say to another person is that "I am grateful for having you in my life, and I appreciate you for who you are." The cards, emails, and text messages that I sent to my IKWC Sister expressed how thankful I was for her positive attitude; words of encouragement; willingness to help; honesty when giving feedback; overall kindness and compassion. When I received expressions of gratitude from my IKWC Sister, she expressed things that she saw in me that I didn't see in myself. Those things pushed me to dig even deeper to be a better me. I thought of the scripture in I Corinthians 12:14-26

(Message Bible), *"Now the body is not one member but many. If the foot should say, "Because I am not a hand I don't belong to the body," does that alter the fact that the foot is a part of the body? Of if the ear should say, "Because I am not an eye I don't belong to the body," does that mean that the ear really is no part of the body? After all, if the body were all one eye, for example, where would be the sense of hearing? Or if it were all one ear, where would be the sense of smell? But God has arranged all the parts in the one body according to his design. For if everything were concentrated in one part, how could there be a body at all? The fact is there are many parts, but only one body. So that the eye cannot say to the hand, "I don't need you!" nor, again, can the head say to the feet, "I don't need you!" On the contrary, those parts of the body which have no obvious function are the more essential to health: and to those parts of the body which seem to us to be less deserving of notice we have to allow the highest honour of function. The parts which do not look beautiful have a deeper beauty in the work they do, while the parts which look beautiful may not be at all essential to life! But God has harmonized the whole body by giving importance of function to the parts which lack apparent importance, that the body should work together as a whole with all the members in sympathetic relationship with one another. So it happens that if one member suffers all the other members suffer with it, and if one member is honoured all the members share a common joy."*

Chapter 7: Thankful for You

As sisters, we are all a member of one body. We have a responsibility to honor and love one another and to look for ways to give one another encouragement. Be thankful for your sisters in ministry, because they are a blessing from God! Ask God each morning, "Which sister do You want me to bless with words of thoughtfulness?" God will bring into your path people who need exactly the encouragement and help that you can give to them. I am thankful for the patience, understanding, supportiveness, and love of my sister friends.

R.E.W.A.R.D. Moments

{1} Yes, we know everything we do is to bring Jesus glory. Honestly, do you like receiving thank you cards or notes of appreciation for who you are?

{2} When was the last time a sister in ministry sent you a "thinking of you" note? How did you feel after reading it?

{3} Pray and ask the Lord, "Who can I bless and encourage, today?"

Chapter 7: Thankful for You

R.E.W.A.R.D. Prayer

Father, I thank You for _____.
She has truly blessed my life. When we first met, I would not have imagined the influence she would have on my life as an individual and as a sister in ministry. Dear Lord, show me how I can be a blessing to her. Show me the areas of her life where she needs encouragement. I count it an honor, not only to be partners in ministry, but also her friend. Cause us to have more R.E.W.A.R.D. experiences together. Forever grateful.

Amen.

R.E.W.A.R.D.

Restoring Every Woman's Adrenaline Rush to Disciple

Chapter 8: *You are My Gift*

We closed the year with a festive Christmas celebration at a charter member's home. One by one, the women presented a gift to the woman whose name they had selected, previously. As each woman presented the gift, she stated how the other woman had been a gift to her throughout the year. The words spoken were sincere and heartfelt. We had an enjoyable night of GOOD food and fellowship. We laughed and we shared fond memories of the year.

My Reflection
By YC

It was awesome to see all the women come together to fellowship and celebrate one another. The conversation was lively, the music was soothing, and the food was plentiful and delicious. The women presented gifts to each other which they felt were meaningful to the person. Who doesn't like receiving a gift? However, this was different.

It wasn't about the gift itself, nor was it about the price of the gift; it was about the person to whom the gift was being presented. To hear the words of why you are a gift to someone, truly warms your heart. We should never underestimate the power of our words or our actions. With one small gesture, you can change a person's life. I encourage you to think about things you can say or do to uplift someone, and make them feel like they are a gift to you. Take good care of those very special people in your life.

God has sent them to you to take special care of you. Celebrate them as the gifts they are and never

Chapter 8: You are My Gift

take them for granted. Always remember to tell them that you love them because you can't tell the people you love how much you love them too often.

R.E.W.A.R.D. Moments

{1} Are you an exhorter or gift-giver? How often do you seek ways to encourage another woman in ministry? List the last thing you did for a woman in ministry and the outcome.

{2} Is there a woman in ministry who is a gift to you? Send her a "you are my gift" card. Pray and ask the Lord what to say and how to deliver it.

Chapter 8: You are My Gift

R.E.W.A.R.D. Prayer

Father, just as You sent Jesus to be a Gift to all mankind, I thank You for the gift of sisterhood. I thank You for the women You have placed in my life. I probably do not say it often to my sisters in ministry, but they are a GIFT to me. And I pray that I am a GIFT to them. Remind me, Lord, every day to appreciate my sisters. Help me not to take for granted the relationships that You have allowed us to establish. Help us to restore one another's adrenaline rush to disciple.

Amen.

R.E.W.A.R.D.

Restoring Every Woman's Adrenaline Rush to Disciple

Chapter 9: *Restored to Disciple*

Matthew 11:28 says, *"Come unto me, all ye that labour and are heavy laden, and I will give you rest."* Rest in the Greek means to refresh, to take ease. So many times as women, we feel like, if we are not in the heart of things, the work will not get done. Unfortunately, we carry that same mindset in ministry. That's why we are stressed out, burned out, and tired. We have been raised to be life-givers, caregivers, and nurturers. As women, we have been taught that relationships with other women are dangerous and detrimental to our well-being. Unfortunately, these are the reasons why so many women in ministry are suffering with depression and loneliness. They don't know how to relax and, much less, relate to one another.

We, women in ministry, do not take the time to receive the same care that we give to our families and parishioners. It is not until our bodies breakdown or we receive a bad health report from the doctor that we stop and rest. It is not until we have wounded God's sheep and caused them to turn away from the Father that we come to realize…Restoration is needed. There is a saying, "Hurt people hurt people." But Galatians 6:1a says, "…*restore such an one in the spirit of meekness*…"

The more time you take to rest and to be restored, the more effective you will be in discipling God's sheep.

Yes, the harvest is plenteous and the laborers are few. But even Jesus took time to steal away and be refreshed by His friends, God the Father and God the Holy Spirit. After that time away, He was able to go back and pour Himself into the disciples. He was able to teach and show them the things of God. Throughout scripture, you saw Jesus do GREAT & MIGHTY things after His time of refreshing. He healed a demon-possessed boy; called Peter to walk on water; taught the disciples the importance of prayer & forgiveness; and the list goes on and on.

My dear sisters in ministry, I hope after reading these chapters, honestly answering the *R.E.W.A.R.D. Moments* questions, and reciting the *R.E.W.A.R.D. Prayers* that you too will seek to have a *R.E.W.A.R.D.*

Chapter 9: Restored to Disciple

experience. I hope from this book that you see "God's REST" in so many forms. Yes, a proper amount of sleep is needed. But also, laughter brings rest and refreshment as well. Remember: *"A merry heart doeth good like a medicine."* *(Proverbs 17:22)*

R.E.W.A.R.D.!

About the Developer

Rev. Sharon D. Jones is the devoted wife of Dr. Aaron R. Jones. She enjoys building the Kingdom of God with her husband and pastor. Sharon is the Human Resource Administrator for New Hope Church of God and New Hope Kiddie Kollege daycare in Waldorf, Maryland. She serves as the ministerial liaison for New Hope's Women of the Kingdom ministry. Sharon preaches and facilitates worship services at the D.C. Corrections Corporation of America for Women with the "Glory Chasers" Prison Ministry. She serves as Vice President of the International Kingdom Women's Coalition, Inc. (IKWC) in Upper Marlboro, Maryland. She serves on the Women's Discipleship Board for the Church of God DELMARVA-DC region. Her motto is "Enjoying Life in Christ."

International Kingdom Women's Coalition, Inc.

IKWC is a collage of individual women who willingly come together (both nationally and internationally) to serve and be served by taking each other's vision to the next level. In doing so, we form relationships we may otherwise have never had the opportunity to begin.

How to contact us:

By Mail
IKWC, Inc.
PO Box 1822
Upper Marlboro, MD 20773

By Phone
Voice: 301-218-0820
Fax: 301-218-0819

By Internet
Email: ikwcinc@gmail.com
Website: www.ikwcinc.org